T0094704

following the dog down
(an intimacy of nematodes)

FOLLOWING THE DOG DOWN
(AN INTIMACY OF NEMATODES)

John Liles

OMNIDAWN PUBLISHING
OAKLAND, CALIFORNIA
2017

© Copyright John Liles, 2017. All rights reserved.

Cover illustrations by Brooke Weiland

Cover text set in Gil Sans, Franklin Gothic, and Bell Gothic
Interior text set in Franklin Gothic and Adobe Jenson Pro

Cover and Interior Design by Sharon Zetter

Offset printed in the United States
by Edwards Brothers Malloy, Ann Arbor, Michigan
On 55# Glatfelter B18 Antique
Acid Free Archival Quality Recycled Paper

Library of Congress Cataloging-in-Publication Data

Names: Liles, John, 1991- author.
Title: Following the dog down : an intimacy of nematodes / John Liles.
Description: Oakland, California : Omnidawn Publishing, 2016.
Identifiers: LCCN 2016045483 | ISBN 9781632430366 (pbk. : alk. paper)
Classification: LCC PS3612.I36 A6 2017 | DDC 811/.6--dc23
LC record available at https://lccn.loc.gov/2016045483

Published by Omnidawn Publishing, Oakland, California
www.omnidawn.com   (510) 237-5472   (800) 792-4957
10 9 8 7 6 5 4 3 2 1
ISBN: 978-1-63243-036-6

CONTENTS

On FOLLOWING THE DOG DOWN by John Liles

Rae Armantrout

John Liles' poems are not much like anything being written now. But if you can think of Francis Ponge and Susan Howe at the same time, you begin to get a sense of what he is doing. It's almost as if Francis Ponge had "taken the side" of smaller, more destructive things—but Liles' poems seem less staged than his. *Following the dog down* is a study of and a song for parasitic round worms, sometimes known (suggestively) as "heart worms." In a way, this is about intimacy, what it means that we figuratively and literally consume one another.

Like Susan Howe, Liles is an archival poet. For this poem sequence, he has mined language from 19th- and early 20th-century science writing, often by amateur scientists who studied what they loved. This love for the subject matter (infestation) is part of what I meant by intimacy above. We've all heard the phrase "strange yet familiar." Liles' work is more like familiar yet strange. It's not easy to distinguish self from other when it's "worm by worm / the hunger / you hear back from." The poem dissolves the distinction between parasite and host and between the metaphorical and literal. Here we "touch / the little atom / of someone else's / arrival"

Once habitable homebody
had kept the nest sites
          fed and always
yours.

But who is this "homebody" and, for that matter, who are you? This poem might be seen as a love song to a wholly permeable and dissolving "you."

I was always on my way
to meet you
in amity, unnamable
enthusiasm
blossomed unmending

The lovely set of "m"s and "n"s in those lines form a clasp, an innocent, toxic embrace. The best part of it is that Liles isn't trying to shock you or creep you out, though your skin *may* crawl a bit. He is too far inside his subject for that—or it is too far inside him. Liles' book is very strange and completely sincere. I say this as high praise.

for John Granger

because of Tess Carroll

(touch)

*

the little atom
of someone else's

arrival

and a honeybee's

worth of voltage

that you left out

(to ignite the animal's engines)

utmost long worms

kissing you goodbye

*

(slender filamentous)

*

(the dog's heartworm)

inoculate lung lovers into a scene of longing,
larval arrivals stir in muscle, woundless

subcutaneous months-long migration
until your imagoes jump
blood to go home to the heart

        chew chew little filarial :

                              oblivion ache

           and its ambition
           (myointimal)
           hope teasing us

(to eat easy honey)

come collaterals in red swell
and string further, hot-float
at heart's unrest and love :

live birth prebabies

(new belongings)

the dog heart still tries :

larval company tease
the lung to lesions

accommodated in all at-reach arteries,
prolific threaded perils, heart-skips slugged

into an engine
and a lover
(in the long-term)

the dog we wanted longer
and chewed through,
chanced together to
our endpoint
and at last at capacity :

further your ambition
to knot, and I no longer
have a heart for this

*

(mum bustle of)

*

to remain gently,
　　　　attending
　　　　your weary, flinching other

our teeth delayed scaping

　　　　　soft gnaws : slow corolla

　　　　　　　　bloom,
　　　　　　　　brigandage

　　　　　　　　or shoot the stomach,

　　　whenever the wednesday

*

(nemobius trip)

*

gallant and gutless
        horsehair courters
with hopes of manipulating crickets

parasites who've realized
        their motherly impulse

                then went pearling
                lakeside promises

                                        (eating these eggs accidently)

residential chirpers swallow

their own endpoints :

                invading infants who've
                commandeered viscera

and their tremendous knots
erupt from host exoskeletons

        like houseguests,

                     her daughters

        and the crickets
        driven, enamored to,

        will attend them
        all the way to water

*

(saw it down)

*

gaslighting romantics

    who speak sweetly
    and affect lesions

nearly innocuous palm-sized grifters
    stay undetected
    antigens
    in a host body

your human machinery mistaken :

    nematodes unrecognized
    as non-self and their bedsides
    attended,
                you've thrown blankets

like limpets embracing boulders

contagious heartworms with you always :

gentle disasters entombed

in your honey

(larval toxocara)

*

in young lagomorphs

areas of coagulative necrosis,
                fibrosis

            and focal hepatitis

                        raise white spots on the liver

(ulcers of novel cottontails are more pronounced)

*

(a. necator)

*

lungs we observed hemorrhaged

larvae lay free in the tissues
and were not associated with

against intact skin : the typical worm-like hollows

(otherwise harmless)
hookworms might snowball embolus,
dead-end knots toward blossomed

respiration in a living byway,
pneumonia in very young pups
is symptomatic, a last chance

migrans in man is the toxocara dog ascarid :

your creeping eruption of larval crawlers

*

(little s. stilesi)

*

spring lambing, cotton
flock sought anectdotal
domestics, animal meat

new allopatry in autumn,
the emerging ecotones
sprung of young mutton

lungworm assemblages
occurring in the parenchyma
of ovis throughout the world

stateside found in all lambs
six months and over
sent to slaughter

*

(d. tenuis)

*

with a denticulate touch
                    alighting needles,
                    two fetal bones

calluses in alveoli,

                    gut accessories
                    and their ocular lumen
                              lag

                    worms encysting
                    host-cell necrosis

              an ovine unnoticeably
              consuming herself

      (infected animals generally show no signs of disease)

*

(a. suum)

*

mouthlike appendages :

      buccal embracers
      efflorescing
shark teeth

sprint, fanatical
      flatworms
of half-dead drifts
where pigs with
their mouths open
touch pneumonia
      (nose-to-nose)

      and are downed
      before slaughter

*

(this together)

*

low little carnivore causing
            further hearts

    in the homebody

    while I eat and am eaten
    to survive my body longer
    in the mouths of others

        (you cannot stay unloved in this)

            and we're all hurting

*

(t.axei)

*

innumerate, incite cushions
in a companion animal

localizing the empties in each
progressive nesting   (organ)

to pair risky thickenings
in the stomach   (fundus)

(or cause the horse to colic)

you were a longshot into digestive acids :

fraught longer into lumen,
lost shoulders and gone knots

                (erosion present in severe or longstanding cases)

*

(stay)

*

your endurance is a landslide

(long-over)

fresh salt
        until we have left

*

(c.punctata)

*

(calves experimentally infected)

mostly confined to the duodenum

and consisted of catarrhal
inflammation with a fine
fibrous necrotic exudate

hemorrhages
and thickenings
(of the intestinal wall)

in serosa and mucosa

oh sacred rattlesnakes

(tacit sensations in your hindgut)

*

(as long as you could)

*

worm by worm
the hunger
you hear back from

(what it is to cherish another)

wager all starving on them

(and how we understand when you let up)

*

(nonesuch and moony)

*

flippant and chewy you
exacting that sort of sympathy

miss me my absent affect

to want to be a part of this

(even after we have both left home)

*

(bolt)

*

having affixed your every
living loved-one, our

once-habitable homebody
had kept the nest sites
        fed and always
yours, an only hope

        the worm burdens
        with care that couldn't
        mollycoddle

        and destitute
                        your linchpin ancestral
        dog gone,

                        endogenous planetesimal
seedlings,   rockets
into an afterglow

*

(an animal was always)

*

and if even with all lost we all
have our end-points

I was always on my way to meet you

*

(took so much)

*

softer connections go ball and socket

touch articulating and all
that you squeeze into

(a touchstone)
turns in taciturn,
attempted to chew little

floaty, almost innocuously

in amity, unamenable
enthusiasm
blossomed unmending   traumas

summer sore horses
and the gut blind tyros
caught adoring them

(home)

because I asked for help
and was helpless

                    here I am harming
                          you

                          *

(r. ocypodis)

*

             the overridden lithosphere
of an animal
      smashmouthed

      freelancers
      spontaneously
      pearling underbellies

      until a commensalist's last
      calcium scrapping toward
      a wedding day

      endurant and an obligate
      constituent
      of charm

(to bloom someone else's ornamentals)

a sympathetic landlord,
their prevailing
nosebleeds

and somehow
this feels like
too much

*

(when leaving, when left)

*

but I wouldn't want to remain here
and I have damaged the heart of this

my wandering substrate
my motion towards

*

ACNOWLEDGMENTS

My deep and underspoken appreciation must be given to Tess Carroll, Rae Armantrout, John Granger, Thalia Field, Ben Doller, Emily Means, Beata Kasiarz, Ben Luton, Isabel Balée, Desiree Bailey, Peter Geibel, Teri Havener, Ben Stillerman, every teacher who took the time for me, every coach who stayed late so that I could work further, and to you, for taking this moment to listen.

Further gratitude is owed to those who have taken such great care and consideration while shaping this work throughout the bookmaking process: Rusty Morrison, Ken Keegan, Gillian Hamel, Sharon Zetter, Cameron Stuart, and Brian Teare—to whom I will forever be enormously grateful, the one to first bring my work to light.

With tremendous apology to Tess Carroll, whose heart I inflicted unforgivably in the company of my care, and who was endurant beyond reason in carrying this burden to its end.

RECOMMENDED FURTHER READING REGARDING THE SCIENCE OF NEMATODES (ROUNDWORMS) :

Works available in the public domain :

The collected volumes of Contributions to a Science of Nematology, by N.A. Cobb, the Father of Nematology (1914 – 1935)

An Introduction to Nematology, by B. G. Chitwood and M.B. Chitwood (1937)

Modes and forms of Reproduction of Nematodes, by E. Maupus (1900)

Principles of Nematology, a source of beautiful illustration, by Gerald Thorne (1961)

Delightfully informative, and relatively present-day, texts :

Nematode Parasites of Vertebrates: Their Development and Transmission, by Roy C. Anderson (2000)

Nematode Parasites of Domestic Animals and of Man, by Norman D Levine (1980)

For general parisitology, among the many expert texts, the author recommends :

Parasitology: The Biology of Animal Parasites, by Elmer R. Noble (first published in 1962, with many updated versions)

JOHN LILES is a poet, science writer, and living mammal. His written work aims at establishing further interdisciplinary spaces for the arts and sciences, and he is continually invested in collaborating with students, researchers, and academics to facilitate new expressions of expertise from the forefronts of expertise. Sections of this chapbook have been included as course material for Writing for the Sciences Workshops at the University of San Diego, California. Other work has appeared in *Arcadia, inter/rupture, decomP,* and *Gulf Stream Literary Review,* and has received the Ina Coolbrith Memorial Poetry Prize and the Stewart Prize for Poetry. On a good day, he's a dog and we don't need to overthink it.

Following the dog down (an intimacy of nematodes)
by John Liles

Cover illustrations by Brooke Weiland

Cover text set in Gil Sans, Franklin Gothic, and Bell Gothic
Interior text set in Franklin Gothic and Adobe Jenson Pro

Cover and interior design by Sharon Zetter

Offset printed in the United States
by Edwards Brothers Malloy, Ann Arbor, Michigan
On 55# Glatfelter B18 Antique
Acid Free Archival Quality Recycled Paper

Publication of this book was made possible in part by gifts from:
The New Place Fund
Robin & Curt Caton

Omnidawn Publishing
Oakland, California
2017

Rusty Morrison & Ken Keegan, senior editors & co-publishers
Gillian Olivia Blythe Hamel, managing editor
Cassandra Smith, poetry editor & book designer
Sharon Zetter, poetry editor, book designer & development officer
Liza Flum, poetry editor & marketing assistant
Peter Burghardt, poetry editor
Juliana Paslay, fiction editor
Gail Aronson, fiction editor
Cameron Stuart, marketing assistant
Avren Keating, administrative assistant
Kevin Peters, *OmniVerse* Lit Scene editor
Sara Burant, *OmniVerse* reviews editor
Josie Gallup, publicity assistant
SD Sumner, copyeditor
Briana Swain, marketing assistant